3

DESIGNER'S GUIDE TO JAPANESE
PATTERNS

JEANNE ALLEN

Original book concept
by Takashi Katano

CHRONICLE BOOKS ■ SAN FRANCISCO

■ CONTENTS

**First published in the United States 1989
by Chronicle Books**

English text copyright © 1989 by Chronicle Books

Copyright © 1987 by Kawade Shobo Shinsha
Publishers. All rights reserved. No part of this book
may be reproduced in any form without written
permission from Chronicle Books.

Printed in Japan.

Oh-cho Mon-yo Jiten by Takashi Katano was first
published in Japan by Kawade Shobo Shinsha
Publishers.

Library of Congress Cataloging in Publication Data:

Allen, Jeanne, 1945-
    Designer's guide to Japanese patterns. 3 / Jeanne
Allen; original book concept by Takashi Katano.
        p.   cm.
    Based on: Ōchō mon 'yō jiten / Takashi Katano.
    Bibliography: p.
    ISBN 0-87701-606-2 (pbk)
    ISBN 0-87701-611-9 (cloth)
    1. Decoration and ornament–Japan–Themes,
motives. I. Katano, Takashi, 1934- Ōchō mon 'yō jiten.
II. Title.
NK1484.A1A46 1989
745.4'4952–dc19   89-941
                                                       CIP

Edited by Terry Ryan
Cover design by Karen Pike
Translation by Aiko Yasutomo
Typesetting by TBH Typecast, Inc.

Distributed in Canada by Raincoast Books,
112 East Third Avenue, Vancouver, B.C., V5T 1C8

10 9 8 7 6 5 4 3 2 1

Chronicle Books
275 Fifth Street
San Francisco, California
94103

■ INTRODUCTION

On a recent trip to Japan, I found myself being interrogated by the young and aggressive president of a Japanese trading company who desperately wanted information on new American market trends. When I jokingly protested the Japanese lack of originality in developing their own products, he said, ''You don't understand our business way. It is the work of our company members to go out to America and Europe and find some good thing, then bring it back to Japan so we can improve it. Then, finally, you will like it even better than before.''

This precise and heartfelt summation of the Japanese business genius of the last quarter of the twentieth century also accurately describes the cultural and artistic genius of the Heian period more than a thousand years earlier. Popularly regarded as the golden age of Japan, the Heian period (794–1185) began as a carbon copy of China's elegant T'ang dynasty (618–906) and ended as a culturally independent society whose artistic achievements and originality still awe the rest of the world.

The brilliant T'ang dynasty was a glorious time for artistic pursuits— painting, music, calligraphy, and poetry flourished. The Japanese must be admired for their discrimination and good taste in first identifying, then adopting, and finally refining the best aspects of T'ang culture. The first contact with China occurred in the Nara period (710–794), and by the time Japanese Emperor Kammu had moved the chrysanthemum throne from Nara to Heian-kyō (now Kyoto) in 794 to escape the bigotry and intrigues of the Buddhist priests, his court had developed a seemingly insatiable appetite for all things Chinese.

Chinese monks, intellectuals, and artists—as well as merchants and government officials—were enthusiastically received and emulated by the Heian court. Heian dignitaries, in turn, visited T'ang China, as did young Japanese scholars and courtiers, who regarded the pilgrimage as the final stage of their education.

Although smaller, Heian-kyō was an otherwise exact replica of the T'ang capital of Ch'ang-an and perfectly accommodated the emperor and the several hundred nobles that made up his court. The Heian world outside the imperial city existed but was considered a barbaric netherland to be avoided at all costs. For a Heian patrician, the worst possible punishment was banishment from the charmed, peaceful circle of the imperial compound.

The guardians of Heian-kyō's tranquility were provincial warrior tribes, such as the Taira (Heike) and Minamoto (Gengi) clans. But because these defenders were considered almost subhuman, their services were rarely noted, let alone rewarded. (This snobbery ultimately proved fatal for the aristocrats, who eventually lost everything to the military they had used and despised.)

For the elite surrounding the Heian throne, life focused exclusively on aesthetic pursuits. The business of being an aristocrat required a mastery of poetry writing, calligraphy, and music. Elegance and sensitivity in all things—especially dress and manners—were essential for living within the court. Administrative duties and politics had low priorities in an environment ruled by beauty, so statecraft, like war, was delegated to others—once again to the detriment of the throne.

In spite of their over-refinement and narrow attitudes, the Heian aristocrats' emphasis on cultural accomplishments stimulated an outpouring of artistic treasures that gave this golden age of Japan its justly deserved name.

By the ninth century, the glory of the T'ang dynasty began to fade, as did the interest of the Heian court in life outside the walls of Heian-kyō. Bored with their Chinese-look-alike lives, the aristocrats began a process of modification and refinement that was to continue uninterrupted for 300 years, until a perfectly crafted Japanese aesthetic had been fully realized. So distinct was this new Heian look that Japanese painting with Japanese subject matter came to be known as *yamato-e*, to distinguish it from *kara-e* (painting with a Chinese theme). Most of the thematic and stylistic qualities we now associate with Japanese culture—banks of elegant irises, flowing streams, pristine images of the four seasons, dramatic clouds of black birds soaring diagonally across the picture plane—are products of the Heian legacy.

Women of the Heian court exerted more influence than their Chinese T'ang counterparts, largely because they were used to extend and infiltrate (by marriage) Heian family power cliques. The Fujiwara family, principal suppliers of imperial consorts during most of the Heian period, acquired power primarily through their women. By the middle of the ninth century, the throne and the era began to be called the Fujiwara-Heian period because most emperors had been born to Fujiwara mothers and had married Fujiwara wives.

Being active, powerful members of the court, the women had enthusiasm and an appetite for cultural pursuits equal to the men's. Unfortunately, the male-oriented Chinese writing system of ideographs known as *kanji* was unsympathetic to the female gender and inadequate to express their intensely romantic moods. To remedy this situation, the women of the court embraced and developed a new written language known as *kana*, a 48-character syllabary introduced by Buddhist priest Kōbō Daishi at the encouragement of Emperor Kammu. The *kana* syllabary—often cited as the most important achievement of the Heian period—freed Japanese calligraphy from total reliance on Chinese writing. Initially used exclusively by women to express the intimacies of domestic life, *kana* was used first to produce diaries and *waka* poetry. Since men needed to know *kana* to have any social or romantic dealings with women, the new language was an immediate success, relegating *kanji* to the tedious matters of politics and government.

The importance of *kana* calligraphy to the development and preservation of Heian culture cannot be overstated. Much of what we know about the society comes from the diaries, narrative handscrolls (*emaki-mono*), and novels (*monogatari*) of the period. The most famous work of the period is *The Tale of Genji*, a late-tenth-century novel about the courtly life and loves of the charming Prince Genji, written by Lady Murasaki Shikibu, a member of the same elitist society. Now considered a national treasure, *Genji* breathes color into a history whose only tangible heritage consists of faded, tattered handscrolls and fragments of once-beautiful brocades.

We know from Lady Murasaki's narrative that hers was a polygamous society in which marriages were always arranged —usually for reasons of politics or pedigree. Once the requisite heir was born, however, both partners were free to engage in multiple liaisons. Unless the bride moved to the court, she rarely left her parents' home, so marital status was often a formality of bloodline.

Heian society was so intensely narcissistic that its artistic output seems all the more formidable. The social responsibilities of the aristocrats were so time-consuming and demanding that they could have had little time for other interests. To complicate matters further, the aristocrats' abhorrence of direct confrontation necessitated an elaborate system of protocol decipherable only to the elite. The mannered, other-worldliness of court life was made even stranger because it was lived at night in dimly lit tatami rooms divided by fragile painted screens. Because of the screens, suitors rarely saw the heavily painted white faces and black-lacquered teeth of the women they romanced. It was considered more provocative to identify a loved one by her scent or the variegated colors of the 20 silk kimonos she wore beneath brocaded outer robes.

A woman usually wore her court dress for several days at a time, not removing it even to sleep. Both she and her clothing were heavily scented, not simply to avoid being offensive but to be identifiable to any suitor properly educated in the niceties of court.

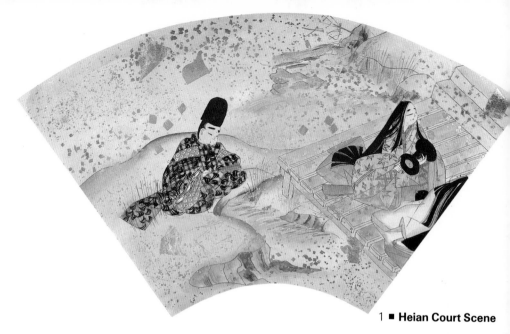

1 ■ **Heian Court Scene**

Covetous of the women's sumptuous dress, the men of the court began to adopt equally elaborate costumes. Face powder, rouge, and scent became fashionable for men. By the mid-Heian period, men's dress became so cumbersome that there was very little room for moving about.

Since mobility had become a problem and direct communication a social taboo, the preliminary work of courting was done through the passing of *waka* poetry. These 31-syllable poems owed their existence to *kana* script and were consequently an original product of the time. Allegedly composed in moments of heightened sensitivity, *waka* poems were considered the perfect instruments for communicating the subjective emotions of love. The poems were crafted to display a lover's cleverness and *mono-no-aware* (sensitivity to the transient and sad beauty of life)—the most highly regarded emotion of the culture.

The finest examples of the tremendous outpouring of *waka* poetry were exquisitely penned onto handscrolls known as *emaki-mono*, which combined *waka*, *ryōshi* (decorated papers), and *yamato-e* (painting with a Japanese theme). The making of *emaki-mono* was an important social activity, a joint effort that combined the color and composition skills of the aristocratic painting masters (*eshi*) and the finishing work of the court artisans.

While many of the patterns in this book come from early textiles and lacquerware, the majority were first used as background designs for *emaki-mono*. The designs were laid down on the *ryōshi* using stenciling or rubbing techniques. The papers were then decorated with mother-of-pearl, bits of mica, and gold or silver paint. After this decoration had set, the paintings were added and narrative or poetry was written on the paper in spidery *kana* calligraphy.

The patterns seen here from the Nara and early Heian periods are clearly either copies of Chinese works or thematic adaptations of T'ang art. As the period moves forward and the process of refinement and stylization takes over, a definable delicacy and vitality begin to appear in the designs.

The Chinese, when asked, often express chagrin at the obvious wholesale borrowing of their classical heritage. The Japanese, however, are satisfied that what they borrowed they improved immeasurably—to the benefit of all.

2 ■ **Scattered Trees and Birds**

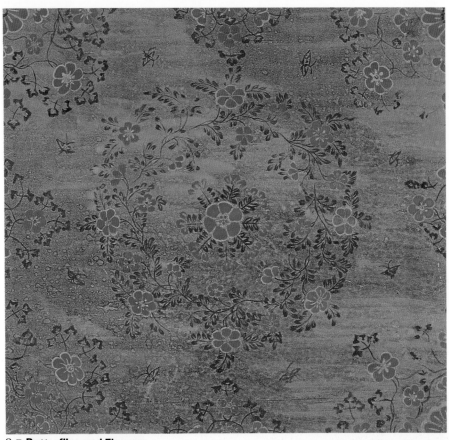

3 ■ Butterflies and Flowers

4 ■ Exotic Fruit in Arabesque

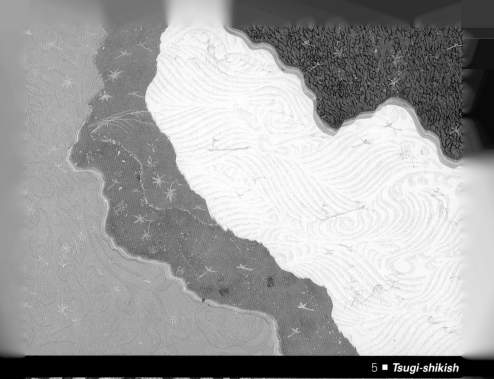

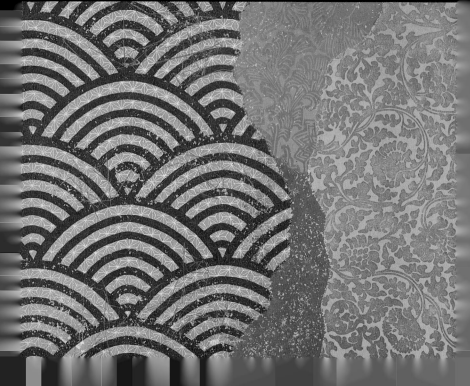

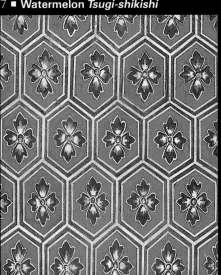

7 ■ Watermelon *Tsugi-shikishi*

8 ■ Tortoise Shell *Hanabashi*

10 ■ Heike Geometric

11 ■ Scrolling Lotus

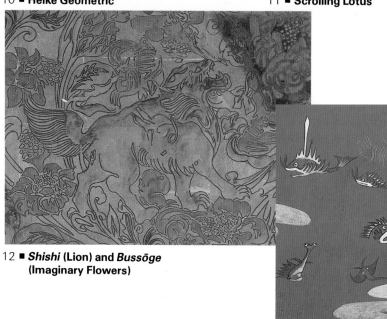

12 ■ *Shishi* (Lion) and *Bussōge*
(Imaginary Flowers)

13 ■ Fish

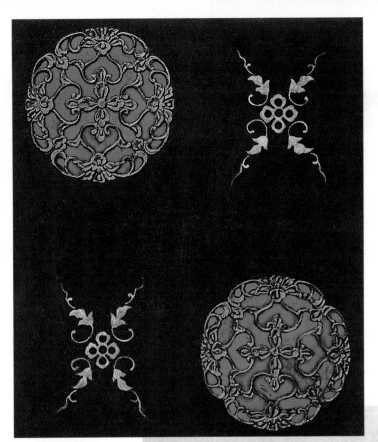

14 ■ **Marquetry Roundels**

15 ■ *Raden Bussōge*

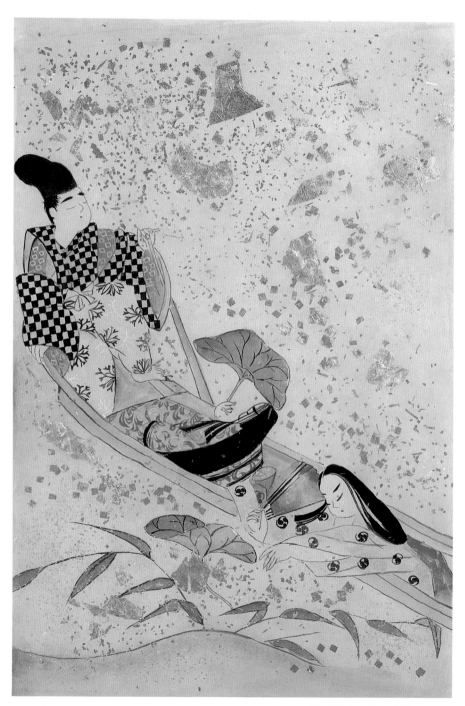

16 ■ **Heian Court Pleasures**

17

18

17 ■ Autumn Flowers

In the Heian period's Fujiwara era (897–1185), Japanese artists began to move away from Chinese influence and toward a distinctively Japanese style. This fine-line composition of autumn flowers and grasses is free from the still-life symmetry and bilateralism typical of Chinese design.

18 ■ Autumn Flowers and Animals

While pre-Heian designs borrowed both their style and subject matter from the Chinese, this later design from *The Anthology of the 36 Poets* is made up of plants indigenous to Japan: *susuki* (pampas grass), *hagi* (bush clover), and *ominaeshi* (a yellow-flowered perennial).

20

19 ■ Thistle *Karakusa* (Scrolling Vines)
Brought to Japan along the silk road from
Persia and routed through India, China,
and Korea, florid arabesque designs such
as this were greatly favored by Heian
artisans for the decoration of ceramics,
lacquer, and textiles.

20 ■ *Ashide* (Hidden Writing) Pattern
Ashide patterns contained hidden writing
in the form of *kana* script that was
ingeniously worked into the painted
composition. *Ashide* was characteristic of
yamato-e—Japanese painting containing
typical Japanese subject matter, such as
the soaring birds in this design.

15

21

21 ■ *Ashibune* (Reeds and Boat)

This design is taken from *The Anthology of Shigeyuki*, one section of *The Anthology of the 36 Poets*, a revered Heian work of art and literature created in 1112 to honor Emperor Toba. The 39 volumes that make up the anthology represent the collective efforts of Japan's major poets and the court's most skilled calligraphers, who executed the works on *ryōshi* (Japanese decorated papers). The anthology remained with the imperial family until the sixteenth century, when it was given to the Nishi Honganji Temple.

22 ■ *Inbutsu* (The Stamp of Buddha)

Sometimes used to stamp paper copies of Buddhist sutras (prayers), this design was (and is today) regarded as an auspicious symbol. The temples used these religious stamps to generate revenue; for a donation, the Heian faithful could buy the hope of good health, many sons, or luck in business. Today, temples are still frequented by the ardent, including the not-so-faithful young known as *shin-jinrui* ("new human beings"), who enthusiastically purchase charms that promise good examination scores or romance.

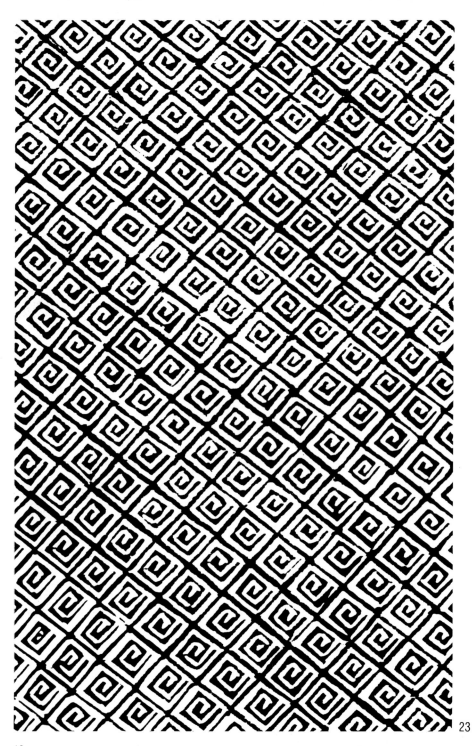

24

23 ■ Woodblock Scroll
While the basic scroll motif was originally borrowed from China, this version has clearly been assimilated and reinterpreted in a recognizably Japanese style. Set on the diagonal and drawn with a free and open hand, this utilitarian design has been used for centuries to decorate textiles.

24 ■ Clouds and Cranes
These floating clouds and cranes were used as the base pattern for the poetry papers of *The Anthology of Hon-amigire*, from *The Anthology of the 36 Poets*. The crane is a traditional good luck symbol and is used to decorate everything from kimono to wrapping paper.

25 ■ Double Roundels and *Karakusa*
This arabesque pattern synthesizes the diverse external influences that combined to create what has become recognized as early Japanese art of the Nara period (710–794). The delicacy and flow of the pattern suggest the artistry to come in the Heian period (794–1185).

26 ■ *Yamato-e* in Roundels
After assimilating a wealth of cultural stimulation during the cosmopolitan Nara period, Japanese artisans of the Heian period turned inward and developed their own artistic idioms. This pattern dispenses with the overused Chinese referents and concentrates on a fresh and elegant simplicity.

27 ■ Roundels and Small, Flowered
Karakusa

Although few fragments of textiles and poetry papers survive from the culturally rich and inventive Heian court, the diaries meticulously kept by court aristocrats describe court life and protocol in intimate detail. It was the job of the courtier to oversee the ceremonies and to docu-ment their every facet—from the positioning of the participants to the clothing they wore—as a guide for the next generation. This design might well have appeared as decoration on one of the ceremonial robes.

28

28 ■ Phoenixes in Roundel and
Karakusa

First introduced into Japan on cloth and
paper printed in the batik (wax-resist)
method, this distinctively Chinese design
is an abstract image of two interlocking
phoenixes. Always an important image in
the decorative arts, the phoenix achieved
its greatest glory as the crowning touch
on the architecturally brilliant Phoenix
Hall, the centerpiece of Byōdōin, the
Fujiwara estate. Completed in 1053, the
estate is considered to be the ultimate
fusion of Heian religious fervor and
aristocratic splendor.

23

29 ■ Phoenixes in Roundels and
   ***Shippō* (Linked Gems)**
The linked gems that form the background of this design are a traditional
Japanese pattern that is still used today
to decorate *obi*, as well as everyday clothing. Elegant roundels add sophistication
and formality to the pattern.

30 ■ Birds in Roundels on Lattice
Edo designers delighted in mixing the
elegant with the mundane to create a
fashion jolt. The seeds of this impulse
may have been planted by the Heian
artisans who created patterns like this
one, floating elegant roundels and exotic
birds on common lattice grids.

31 ■ *Hanabashi* (Flower Diamond Check) in Roundels

Widely used by Heian artisans, *hanabashi* was a favorite decoration for clothing and personal objects. The delicacy and resolution anticipate Kamakura (1185–1338) designs and suggest that the pattern dates from the late Heian period.

32 ■ *Hanabashi* Weavers' Guide

This is a clever adaptation of the pattern guide used by the weavers to execute the difficult roundels. The design has a simple, lighthearted quality that is more akin to the Edo mentality than the Heian, indicating that this was probably a later version of an early court theme.

33

33 ■ Dragons in Roundel

The dragon, an imaginary creature like the phoenix, was adopted by the Japanese from Chinese culture. Symbolic of strength and ferocity, this fire-breathing image was greatly favored by the military during the Kamakura period to decorate clothing and personal implements. This fine-line Heian design, with the dragons rhythmically worked into a triangular motif within the roundel, was probably used to decorate lacquer or textiles.

34

34 ■ Nara Dragons

The obvious Chinese character of this design suggests that it is older than the previous example, perhaps dating back to the Nara period. Here, the dragons are worked like arabesques to create the roundel naturally. Even without the banded perimeter on the pattern, the roundel would be obvious. The wooden, two-dimensional character of the design strongly suggests that the pattern was copied directly from a tapestry imported from China. While the design itself is satisfactory, the execution is uninspired.

36

35 ■ *Momiji* (Maples)

Maple leaves figure largely in both the art and the poetry of the Heian period—colors, shapes, and movement from tree to ground were lyrically recorded in minute detail. Maple viewing and the resulting *waka* poetry were the focus of Heian court life in autumn.

36 ■ Fruit *Karakusa*

Heian artists, tired of overused Chinese themes and unconcerned about authenticity, created their own images of exotic flora and fauna from faraway lands. Although the leaf in this design is adapted from the Japanese banana leaf, the fruit is completely imaginary.

37 ■ Mist and Pine Trees

Heian aristocrats strove for a balance of body and mind, sometimes described as *kokoro*. A person with *kokoro* was sensitive to beauty and life and displayed this quality in actions, in dress, and, perhaps most important, in the writing of poetry. The most elevated poems came in the poet's recognition of an emotion momentarily reflected in nature. This same impulse was translated into art, where poetic moments, such as pines in the mist, became favorite images for the decoration of court robes.

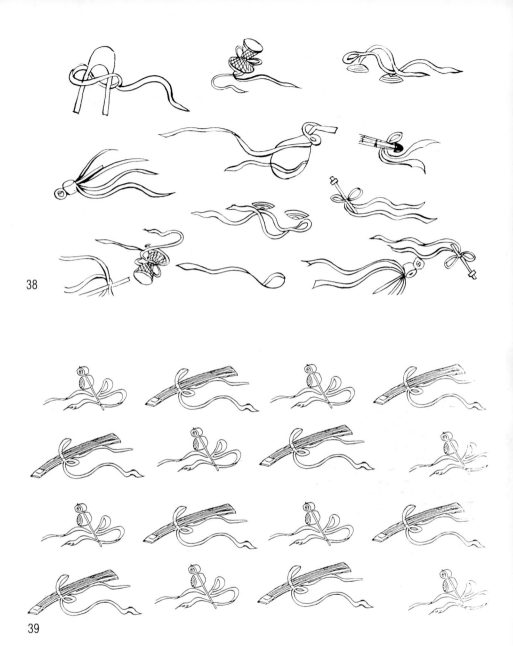

38

39

38 ■ Ancient Musical Instruments

Elegant court music (*gagaku*) was an integral part of the aristocrat's life. All members of the court were expected to be proficient on an array of instruments, including *koto* (a stringed instrument), flute, and *biwa* (lute)—all instruments adopted from the Chinese court.

39 ■ *Gagaku* (Elegant Court Music)

Considering the serious nature of most Heian art, this charming design of traditional musical instruments and floating ribbons is a delightful surprise. The artist has aptly expressed the importance of music in the Heian court and the obvious pleasure it provided.

41

40 ■ Vine *Karakusa*
The immensely popular scrolling vine
patterns came from China as elaborate,
embellished designs. Over time, the
Japanese simplified and refined most
imported patterns to suit their own tastes.
Here, the *karakusa* has been reduced to a
simple vine.

41 ■ *Inkin Karakusa*
One of the reasons for simplifying designs
in the late Heian period was to accommo-
date the popularity of silver and gold foil
embellishments on brocade. For this *inkin*
process, gold leaf is directly applied or
stamped onto the cloth.

42

42 ■ *Sumi-e Karakusa*

This striking design is a black-and-white ink painting (*sumi-e*) that originated as a *maki-e* design on lacquer, in which the motif was defined by sprinkling gold dust on the wet lacquer. This version is surprisingly modern, considering that the image was probably created in the late Heian period. The pattern, which may have decorated a special box or screen, has an enchanting rhythm and flow that identify it as one of the finest of its period.

43

44

43 ■ *Karako* and Flower *Karakusa*
Subtitled "Children in Old Chinese
Garments," this pattern shows *karako*,
blithe spirits borrowed from Chinese fairy
tales and popular characters in Heian
narratives. This particular pattern is
drawn from the poetry papers known as
The Anthology of Kokin Waka (905).

44 ■ *Karako*
Karako, Chinese children, are drawn here
in a clear and easy hand, adding a lighthearted dimension to the design. These
urchins dressed in opulent brocades were
a favorite theme among Heian artists,
who used them as subjects in screen and
scroll decoration.

45

45 ■ *Karyō-Binga*

The *karyō-binga* is an imaginary bird with a sweet and beautiful singing voice that is often mentioned in Buddhist sutras. Such characters were a common part of Heian religious life, which freely mixed Chinese Buddhism with Japanese Shintoism.

46 ■ Diamond-Shaped Links

At first glance, this pattern might resemble a spacy houndstooth perfect for the aggressive clothing of today's 12-year-olds. It is actually a variation of the *matsukawabishi* designs—brightly dyed patterns that were inspired by the diamond shapes on pine cones.

47 ■ Chrysanthemum Roundels
In the mid-Heian period, a double-weaving or jacquard process was developed that allowed artisans to create embroidered and shaded effects in textile designs. In this family crest belonging to the imperial court, positive and negative images emphasize the chrysanthemum in the roundel.

48 ■ *Kikkō* (Tortoise Shells)
Woven patterns like this charming *kikkō* design were, of necessity, geometric in appearance. The hexagonal tortoise shell patterns were one category of *yūsoku*— patterns that were specifically designed for use on the ceremonial garments worn at the Heian court.

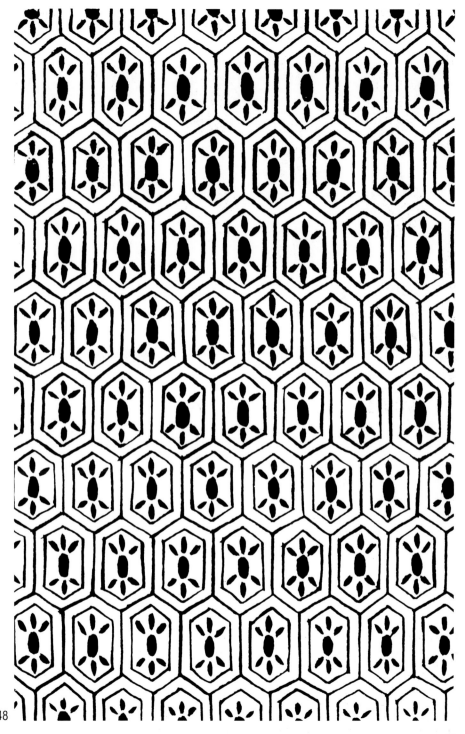

48

49 ■ **Nine-Dot** *Kikkō*

Tortoise shell patterns became very popular among the aristocrats early in the Heian period. These hexagonal lattice patterns often enclosed flower motifs, but here, nine aligned dots form a simple version of the design. This interpretation was probably used as the woven pattern for an aristocrat's outer court robe. The strong geometric simplicity of the pattern has given it the integrity to survive the tides of taste throughout the centuries to the present, where it can still be seen decorating textiles and ceramics.

50

51

50 ■ Tree and Native Plants

In the mid-Heian period, embroidery became a popular decoration for the lavish wardrobes of the extravagant Fujiwara women. Rivaling the fineness of staid woven silks, embroidery often used spare designs like this one to offer an innovative fashion statement.

51 ■ Peacock and *Karakusa*

This design is an adaptation of *kara-nishiki,* a silk brocade woven in China and imported into Japan during the Nara and early Heian periods. Very fashionable among the nobility, *kara-nishiki* was precious and, therefore, used only for the most visible garments or outer wear.

52 ■ *Kōyasan* Twill Pattern

During the reign of Emperor Kammu (781–806), the purer doctrines of Buddhism were emphasized. One of the most revered priests of this period was Kōbō Daishi, who established a cultural center on Kōyasan (Mt. Kōya). Here, priests wove Kōya brocades and silks that were used as covers for court valuables and as mounts for scroll paintings. This simple twill pattern, in which four identical motifs meet at different angles to create a square, was one of the weaving designs used by the Kōya priests.

53

53 ■ Ivy Leaves

During the Heian period, gold and silver embellishment on lacquer, textiles, and ceramics reached the peak of popularity, and the costumes and personal effects of the court aristocracy reflected the finest examples of this extravagance. In this delicate design of cascading ivy leaves, gold foil was artfully stamped onto black lacquer. Even then, the pattern, designed to decorate a box containing the sutras of Heike, was considered a court treasure.

55

55

54 ■ Lotus Flowers in *Maki-e*
Buddhist priests held significant power in
a society where church and state were
not separate. Buddhist art and imagery
thus flowed freely and invaded even the
secular art of the period. This gold leaf
design features Buddhist flowers—some
real, some imaginary.

55 ■ Flower and Plant Splash
Maki-e is a decorating technique developed in the late Heian period in which
metallic dust (in this case, gold) is sprinkled onto wet lacquer to create a design.
While metallics were a popular Chinese
decoration, this particular treatment is
distinctively Japanese.

56 ■ **Pagoda, Clouds, and Dragons**
Another artfully executed design connected with *The Lotus Sutra* of Heike, this
design shows a strong Chinese influence
in its bilateralism and evenly spaced,
well-balanced motifs. In finding its own
identity, Japanese art moved toward a
less conventional use of image and space.

57 ■ **Children and *Bussōge***
This Chinese-inspired design is part of the
great Nara legacy still preserved in
Shōsōin, the imperial repository. The
court treasure contained there, which
includes over ten thousand objects and
personal effects, is our window to the
highly cultured Nara court life.

58

58 ■ Flowers and Butterflies

This romantic, late-Heian design of blossoms, vines, and butterflies is an example of *taka-maki-e*, a process in which the design is created through several applications of gold and silver dust on wet lacquer. The appearance of depth in the design is due to the many stages of lacquering, dusting, and sanding to bring out the surface luster. The subtle shading of the *maki-e* is considered a high point in Fujiwara secular art.

59

59 ■ Comma Shapes and *Karakusa*

Here, in a design borrowed from *The Anthology of the 36 Poets,* is another example of the Heian tendency to meld secular and religious motifs. The Buddhist commas that form the center of the roundels can also be interpreted as drums, an integral part of the *gagaku* (court music) valued so highly by the aristocrats. This particular design is the result of a process called *hira-maki-e,* in which the pattern is created by sprinkling gold dust on tacky lacquer on a clean background.

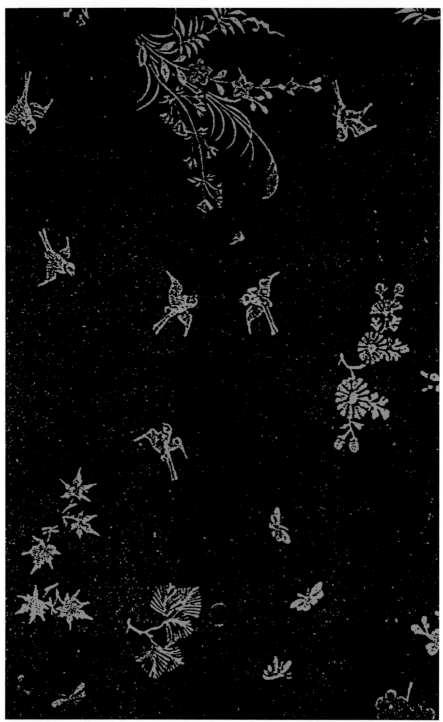

61

60 ■ Birds and Flowering Plants
By the end of the Heian period, Chinese influence in Japanese art was limited to vague, subjective allusions. The entire notion of spatial relationships had moved away from symmetry and obvious order toward the seemingly random but actually planned placement of motifs.

61 ■ Lattice and Flower Shapes
These flower shapes precede the Heian period and were part of a family crest used to decorate the clothing and personal effects of family members. The lattice grids and the diagonal placement of the motifs on the grid create a soft yet strong geometric design.

62

62 ■ Lion and *Karakusa*

This lion design, which was greatly
influenced by Chinese style of the T'ang
dynasty, first appeared on a heavy,
elaborate poetry paper known as *shikishi*.
This example of *shikishi* was part of a
book containing wood engravings that
also used mica in the printing process.

63 ■ *Shippō* Brocade

Composed of roundels and squares, this
design is adapted from a Japanese
brocade (woven) pattern. The Fujiwara
women of the Heian court, who often
wore up to 20 layers of colored silk
kimonos, used such brocades as we
might use jewelry—as accessories to
their costumes.

64

65

64 ■ Trees and Deer

This realistic design adapted from *The Anthology of Ise,* a part of *The Anthology of the 36 Poets,* was drawn with gold and silver on a type of *ryōshi* (decorated Japanese poetry paper). These papers were originally imported from China, then made domestically by court artisans.

65 ■ Island, Waves, and Birds

Known as *kaibu* (a seaside landscape), this unusual design shows an imaginary place where waterplants grow wild on an island in the middle of a frothing sea. The swelling wave pattern is called *kanzeha* and, like *seigaiha* patterns, appears in many Japanese designs.

66

67

66 ■ **Watermelon**

Although there were no watermelons in Japan in the Heian period, the imported motif was a popular one that appeared often on lacquer and as an arabesque design in handscroll paintings. Eventually imported from China, the fruit is now daily fare in the summer.

67 ■ *Zuichō* (Chinese Phoenixes)

This auspicious design of soaring *zuichō* (lucky Chinese phoenixes) probably decorated a chest or small piece of lacquered furniture. Such pieces, beautifully carved and painted with gold and silver by the court artisans, usually originated as part of a bride's dowry.

68 ■ *Zuichō* **and Flower** *Karakusa*
Both birds and blooms in this Chinese fantasy design are imaginary. Like the mythic dragon, the auspicious phoenix was a powerful image borrowed from the Chinese. The phoenix had an important role in every aspect of early Japanese art, music, and literature.

69 ■ *Zuichō* **and Flowering Plants**
Seen flat, this concentric design of swirling phoenixes and flowering plants is slightly dizzying. The image probably made more sense as a decoration on a ceramic vessel; painted in gold on a highly glazed, rounded surface, the design has an engaging energy.

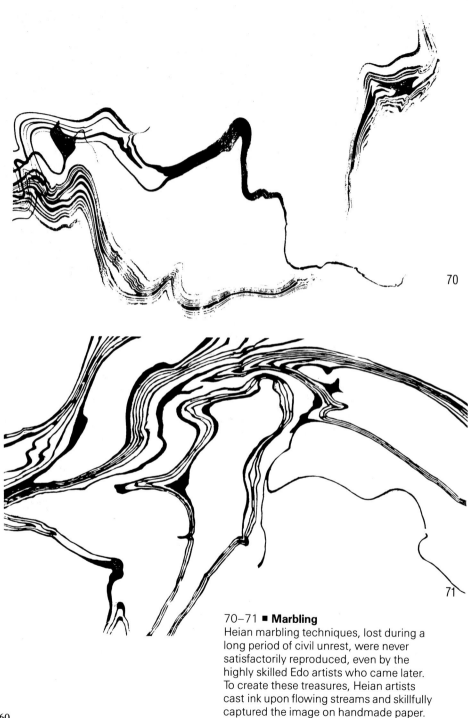

70

71

70–71 ■ Marbling
Heian marbling techniques, lost during a
long period of civil unrest, were never
satisfactorily reproduced, even by the
highly skilled Edo artists who came later.
To create these treasures, Heian artists
cast ink upon flowing streams and skillfully
captured the image on handmade paper.

72

73

72 ■ Sparrow and Bamboo
This charming scene of a sparrow flitting among new bamboo leaves is probably borrowed from an early scroll painting. Unfortunately, most Heian paintings survive today merely as faded fragments, so we can only guess at the original beauty and splendor of their colorings.

73 ■ Bamboo and Birds
Yamato-e (paintings of Japanese subject matter) grew in popularity as *emaki-mono* (narrative picture scrolls) began to grow in importance. The asymmetrical arrangement of motifs across the picture plane marks this mid-Heian handscroll as the work of a native artist.

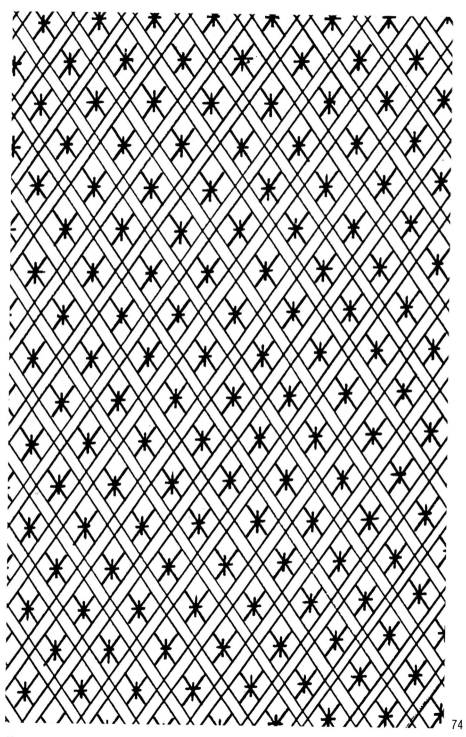

74 ■ Tasuki Hanabashi
Although Edo artists often elevated commonplace images to the level of art, the practice was rare in Heian times. Here, however, the Heian artist has used the everyday *tasuki* (kimono sleeve sash) and abstracted it into a *hanabashi* (flower diamond check) design.

75 ■ Tatewaku (Wandering Stripes)
The *tatewaku* is a design form that has been popular throughout Japanese print history. Probably taken originally from the abstracted image of a wandering stream, the *tatewaku* appears in hundreds of variations and can be regarded as a traditional Japanese stripe.

76 ■ Dandelions
The ordinary dandelion has been transformed in this design into a charming *karakusa* (scrolling vine) pattern, complete with imaginary trailing vines. In the original work, *kana* (Japanese syllabic writing) artfully covered the dandelion arabesque.

77 ■ Flower Lattices
This Escher-like pattern first appears to be a contemporary design of irregular globes or stones set out on the diagonal. To the Heian eye, however, the design is formed with black plovers (small, short-billed wading birds) connected at the wing to make a lattice design.

78 ■ Butterflies
Mid-Heian patterns favored pretty and feminine images such as this. The popularity of this kind of motif increased under the woman-dominated rule of the Fujiwaras. Even the men adopted exaggerated feminine behavior, including the wearing of makeup and jewelry.

79 ■ Scattered Lotus Petals
Originally a sophisticated religious pattern with Buddhist associations, this composition of *chirirengeben* (scattered lotus petals) has become a common domestic design that is often used now to decorate the ordinary necessities of daily life.

80 ■ Fruit and Vine Arabesque

Intricate arabesque patterns like this one were used as backdrop prints to decorate *emaki-mono* (narrative picture scrolls). The most famous *emaki-mono* of the Heian period was *Genji Monogatari (The Tale of Genji)*, a romance of court life written by Murasaki Shikibu in the late tenth century. Much present-day knowledge of Heian court life comes from the careful study of *Genji,* which—unlike the didactic Buddhist tales written for common people—was written by the aristocracy for the aristocracy.

81

81 ■ Ripening Fruit *Karakusa*

This is another *emaki-mono* print. These *karakusa* patterns were often laid down in subtle colors to allow the spidery *kana* script to dance across the design. Color, pattern, and the interplay between the two were of great importance to the aristocracy, who valued aesthetic sensibility above all else. *Mono-no-aware* (a sensitivity to the pathos and transient quality of existence) was the supreme virtue in a society that had more interest in shell games and color matching than in politics and military matters.

82 ■ **Chrysanthemum Vines**
Although Japanese *karakusa* evolved
from imported Chinese patterns, the
astute, robust Chinese versions did not
appeal to the Heian aristocracy, who
preferred more delicate and refined
images. This design is a good example of
the more sophisticated characteristics of
Japanese work.

83 ■ **Islamic Vines**
The symmetry here, the accuracy of the
drawing, and the unusual flowers suggest
that this design was imported from Persia,
via China and Korea. Considered "West-
ern," the design was never altered by the
Japanese, who usually reworked designs
to reflect their own taste.

83

84

84 ■ **Primroses in Arabesque**
Artists might well have combined this
simple, sweet pattern with gold and silver
to decorate a court robe. Since most
social activities were held at night, gold
and silver would not have been gaudy
but totally appropriate for the shadowy
precincts of the court.

85 ■ **Cross-Stitch *Karakusa***
Firefly-catching parties were, according to
The Tale of Genji, a favorite summer
activity of the courtiers. A woman might
have worn a robe decorated with this
floral summer pattern when her suitors
saw her face for the first time lit by the
flickering light of the caged fireflies.

86 ■ Vines and Dandelions
Originally drawn as the background for a
poetry paper, this design is arranged to
emulate the sweep and grace of *kana*
writing, which was developed by the
women of the court. Adopted by the
courtiers, *kana* is often cited as the major
achievement of the Heian period.

87 ■ Children and *Karakusa*
By the mid-Heian period, court artists
were eager to experiment with new techniques and develop new themes. Starting
slowly, they first adapted old themes to
make the new. Here, they have merged
the traditional *karakusa* design with an
unusual motif—children.

88

89

90

88–90 ■ Animal Patterns

Borrowed from jewel-colored carpets brought from the Middle East along the silk route to Japan, these designs show a menagerie of animals that must have seemed fantastic to the Japanese, who had never seen such exotic life before. Such imported works fired the imagina-tion of the Heians, who eagerly incor-porated such animals as the elephant and the zebra into their own mythology. These designs also include imaginary beasts— dragons and phoenixes—as well as the 12 animals of the Chinese calendar.

91 ■ Birds
A design for all times and all seasons, this still-contemporary pattern was a very new image for the Heians. Simple, freely spaced, and crossing the picture plane with an asymmetrical sweep, the design has a realism that sharply breaks with the rigidity and idealism of T'ang art.

92 ■ Bird Twill
This design, seemingly composed of iris blooms in diagonal stripes, is actually an abstraction of birds in flight. (The bird image was probably distorted in the cutting of the screen.) The pattern was expensive to execute, making it all the more attractive to the Heian courtiers.

92

79

93 ■ Birds and Flowering Vines

This is a Chinese-inspired pattern that might have decorated the fragile screens separating the living spaces within the walls of the imperial court. These screens can be seen in the fragments of narrative scrolls that still remain intact. Most of these scrolls had a *fuki-nuki-yaki* perspec- tive (bird's-eye view), so the subjects in the scroll are placed within the gridlike configuration of the screens. Those familiar with court hierarchy can identify the characters by their positions and the kinds and colors of robes they wear.

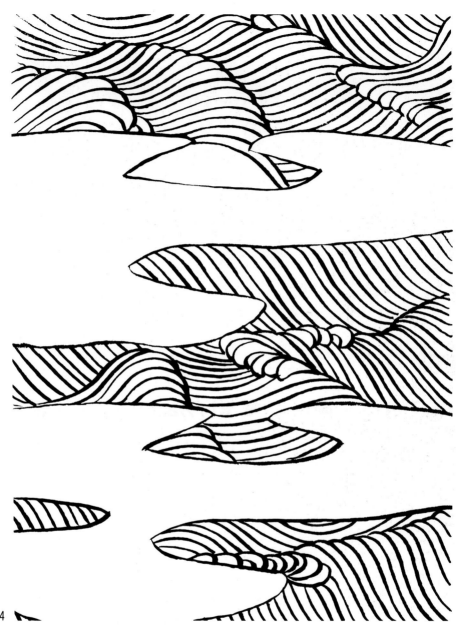

94

94 ■ Waves and Watermarks

Heian works of art on both lacquer and paper often used the device of waves or mist to create space. Several specific wave patterns (*seigaiha, kanzeha*) were stylized to symbolize the sea; abstract patches of mist were created by sprinkling powdered mother-of-pearl onto a wet lacquered surface. In such patterns, the sea and mist are often indistinguishable except for the context. In this design, the wave configuration is apparent, and the negative space between the waves suggests wafting drifts of white mist.

95 ■ Waves and Fish

Amid the swirling waters of this animated *seigaiha* (waves from the blue ocean) pattern are whales and dolphins. This delightful, energetic design was originally painted in bright, clear colors and used as a flyleaf for the Heike *Lotus Sutra*.

96 ■ Tree Peony *Karakusa*

A favorite motif in both China and Japan, the tree peony is used here in arabesque to decorate a sutra cover. Such pious designs give little indication of the constant warring that went on between the power-hungry Buddhist sects and the equally aggressive imperial court.

97 ■ Heike *Lotus Sutra*

In the late Heian period, the most powerful military families were the Taira (also known as Heike) and the Minamoto (known as Genji). As the nobility became increasingly weak and splintered, the two tribes fought one another for control of the court, and the Heike initially prevailed.

Clumsily installed into court life, the Heike adopted aristocratic pursuits with mixed success. Eventually, they were driven out by the Genji, but they left the beautiful Heike *Lotus Sutra,* which this design is taken from, as part of their legacy.

98

98 ■ Double Animals in Roundels

While most *monogatari* (literature) of the time centered on Heian-kyō, didactic tales from India, China, and Korea were also collected by the court literaries. These works introduced a host of exotic characters and fantastic creatures into the Japanese literary tradition. This roundel containing a pair of dragonlike snails probably illustrated an early fairy tale.

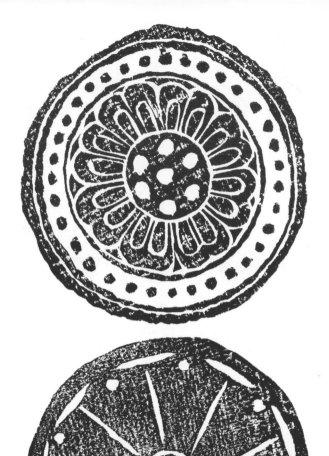

100

101

99 ■ Diagonal *Tasuki*
Resembling a Navajo rug design, this diagonal pattern is an abstraction of *tasuki* (kimono sleeve sash). In later years, the design was called *matsuka-wabishi* (brightly colored diamond-shaped patterns), and the interior diamond was dropped, simplifying the pattern.

100–101 ■ Roof Tiles
Heian aristocrats took great pride in decorating their homes elegantly and fashionably. Every exposed surface, including roof tiles, was embellished. These two designs were taken from tiles custom-designed for a home not a stone's throw from the imperial palace.

102–103 ■ **Hand-Mirror** *Bussōge*

Designed to decorate the backs of two hand mirrors, these roundels are not strictly round but shaped to follow the geometry of an octagon and a hexagon. The importance of hand mirrors to the Heian aristocracy cannot be overemphasized. In this vain society, which was totally obsessed by manners, dress, and makeup, both men and women were essentially married to their mirrors. The fashion of the day mandated heavily powdered faces and necks, painted eyebrows and lips, and blackened teeth.

For all this preparation, however, the

103

aristocrats avoided direct contact with
the opposite sex. Instead, they moved
about in the shadows, believing that the
glimpse of a silken sleeve or the scent
wafting from a noblewoman's long
silken hair was more sensual than a face-
to-face meeting.

104 ■ Peacock Polygon
These geometric weaving patterns are strikingly similar to some of the Indian designs of ancient Mexico and South America. Fantastic animals and bird shapes lent themselves to the blocklike style that could be achieved on looms at that time.

105 ■ Double Animals
In this Chinese-inspired design, the *tasuki* is used at the center of the pattern, with exotic doglike animals facing one another on either side. Unlike some other weaving patterns, this design is not limited to linear use but can spread out to fill the picture plane.

106

107

106 ■ Diamond Waves
This wave pattern, worked to fit within diamond shapes, is often used to decorate the borders of copper utensils and pottery. The cresting wave motif was originally brought from China and is usually associated with heroic sea tales.

107 ■ Hunting Pattern
Structured like an Egyptian frieze, this design shows (top) warriors stalking wild prey with bows and arrows and (bottom) domesticated animals in a pastoral scene. Diamond waves sandwich the two story boards in this private view of Heian every-day life.

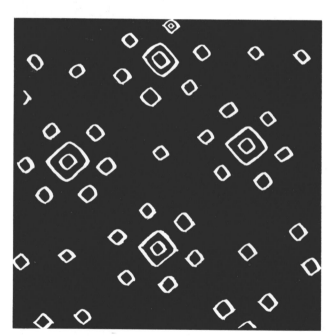

108 ■ Fern Brocade

This fern pattern was especially designed for the highly valued brocade sashes used as accessories in court dress. Brocade strips were also used on outer-robes and to set off hand-held accessories, such as fans or lacquer jewelry.

109 ■ Seven-Days-of-the-Week Stars

Heian *emaki-mono* (picture scrolls) contain many examples of working people dressed in clothes decorated with this star design. Such simple patterns printed in one or two colors were popular among the working classes because they were patterned yet inexpensive.

110

110 ■ Buddhist *Karakusa*

Heian nobles often chose patterns with
Buddhist referents to decorate clothing
and personal objects. Although such
shows of piety were an important aspect
of court life, romance was the preferred
activity, and the art of love made the court
go 'round. A polygamous lot, the
aristocratic men and women married by
political arrangement and, after producing
the mandatory heir, engaged in multiple
amorous liaisons.

111 ■ Vines in Arabesque

This elegant design, although Chinese in feeling, is the work of a Japanese court artisan. Heian culture at its worst was petty, sterile, and overly refined; at its best, it produced outstanding work like this *karakusa*, the quality of which soars past its Chinese antecedent.

112 ■ Floating *Karakusa*

The Heian aristocrat strove to achieve a fusion of art in life and life in art. The laborious cultivation of calligraphy, music, poetry, dress, and manners were all-consuming occupations of the nobility. This *karakusa* has the elements of refinement so admired by this pampered class.

113

114

113 ■ *Kana Karakusa*

This design served as a background for the airy *kana* script that was developed by women in the court for the nobility's domestic and romantic writing. *Kanji* (the Chinese characters) were used for more masculine (political and military) topics.

114 ■ **Arabesque with Exotic Fruit**

Although the Heian court was noted for rejecting foreign cultures, this design is not purely Japanese. The design breaks with Chinese T'ang tradition stylistically, but the imagery composed of exotic fruit and flowers shows that the aristocracy still had a fascination with foreign things.

115

◀ 116

115 ■ Birds Eating Flowers

Emperor Kammu moved Japan's capital from Nara to Kyoto in 794, in part to escape the political stranglehold of the powerful Buddhist sects, but the highly developed cultural achievements of the Nara period—including this hand-mirror design—were brought intact to the new capital.

116 ■ Flower Cars

This design evokes childhood memories of simpler days when four-petaled flowers were fitted with grass stalks to fashion "flower cars." This pattern is a sentimental favorite of the Japanese people who fondly remember life before the time of transformers and computers.

117

117 ■ Flower *Tasuki*

This design is from *The Anthology of the 36 Poets*, a painted narrative that owes its existence to *kana*. The development of *kana* script in the Heian period freed Japan from China's dominating cultural influence. Before the *kana* syllabary, all writing was in Chinese characters known as *kanji*. *Kana*, a phonetic system, was developed by the women of the court, who used the script to write diaries, *monogatari*, and *waka* (Japanese poetry). Only the finest Heian poets were immortalized in *The Anthology of the 36 Poets*.

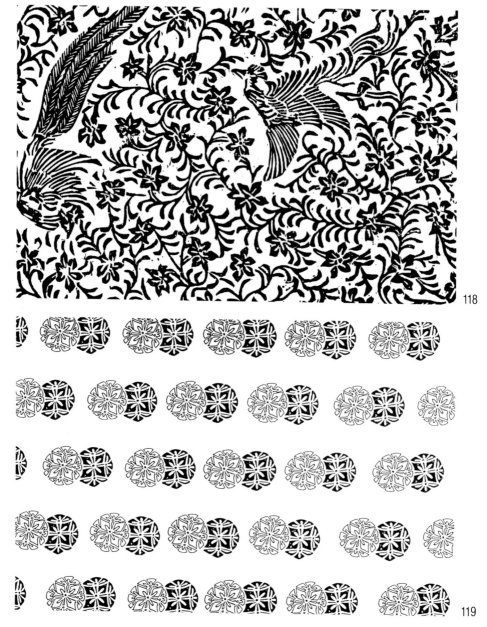

118

119

118 ■ **Flowers and Chinese Phoenix**
This sophisticated and elegant pattern
was first used to decorate both cloth and
metal. Later, it became a popular design
for *ryōshi* (decorated papers). It was
block-printed on *washi,* a paper made
from mulberry fibers, and then decorated
with mica.

119 ■ *Hiyoku Hanabashi*
The idea for *hiyoku* (one design atop
another) originated with an imaginary
pair of flying birds (one male, one female),
each with one eye and one wing. Here,
the *hiyoku* consists of a diamond design
superimposed on *hanabashi* (flower-
shaped motif).

120

120 ■ Flower *Fusenryō*

Fusenryō is an elaborately worked textile. This pleasingly balanced design, which combines flowers within roundels, equilateral triangles, and hexagons, was originally engraved as a block print. The roundel shapes resemble *temari,* the decorative balls that Japanese women make with the brightly colored silk threads left over from the weaving of their kimono.

121

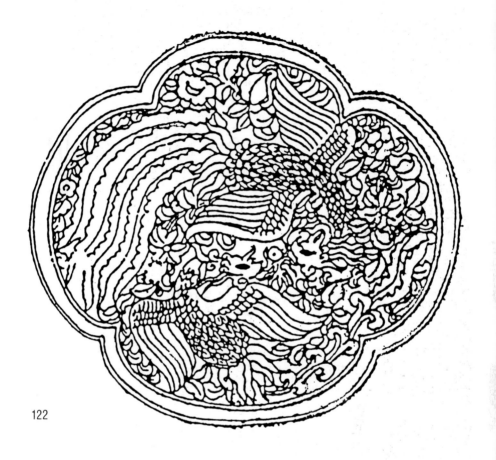

122

121 ■ *Hanabashi Fusenryō*

This elegant design of carefully constructed geometric shapes fashioned from flower and leaf motifs was also achieved by *fusenryō*. Block engraving allowed the artist to make a detailed and intricate design that was beyond the technical reach of Heian stencil makers.

122 ■ **Chinese Phoenix**

Heian aristocrats were highly superstitious and spent much time and energy consulting oracles and chanting sutras. For this reason, they felt it couldn't hurt to adorn their personal effects with such auspicious symbols as the double phoenix shown in this roundel.

103

123

123 ■ Phoenixes, Tigers, and Dragons

In the early Heian period, two new schools of Buddhism—Tendai and Shingon—were added to the six schools that had been so important in Nara. Most aristocrats combined Buddhism with native Shinto beliefs and a spiritual mythology imported from China. Within this religious hodgepodge, animal images—such as those in this roundel—were important talismen with supernatural powers. These personal good luck charms decorated textiles and other household goods.

124

125

124 ■ *Rōsen* Phoenix

Rōsen was a Heian printing technique whereby designs were copied onto hand-made papers. Artists used wax as a rubbing medium to copy woodblock designs onto papers that were probably then used as the background for *waka* poetry.

125 ■ Phoenix and Peony

By setting the two favorite images of the Heian period in an exotic atmosphere, the creator of this design has molded his own idea of heaven. Both the drawing style and the imagery used in this unique *karakusa* made it a favorite textile design of the courtiers.

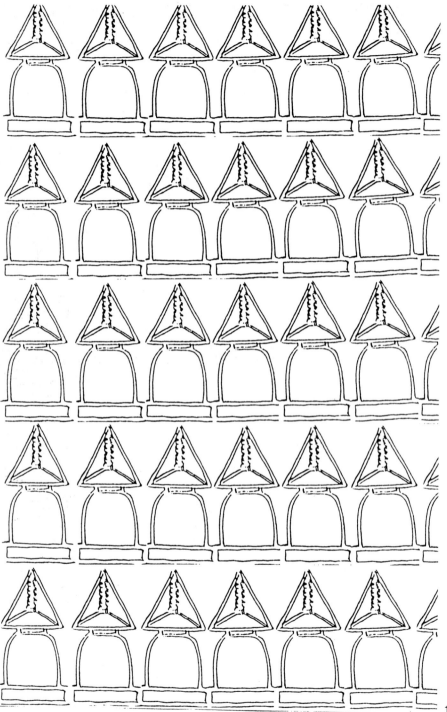

126

127

126 ■ Pagodas

An important Buddhist pattern, this pagoda design was used as the background for special sutras. In this religious version of the *ashide* (hidden writing) patterns, each of the pagoda shapes contain sutra characters ingeniously worked into the composition of the design.

127 ■ Stars

This design was a simple stencil pattern favored by the Heian commoners to decorate their everyday robes. Cost and technique limited their patterns to graphics that appear childlike next to the elaborate *karakusa* of the courtiers, but color offered some variety.

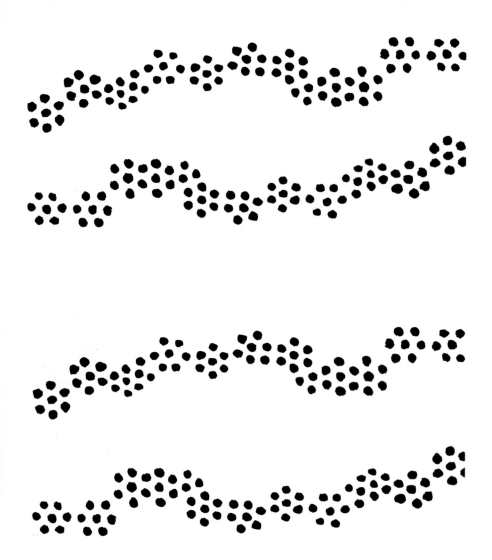

128

128 ■ Linked Stars

Used both in clothing and in the background of narrative scrolls, this charming pattern can still be seen today in traditional Japanese clothing, such as *hanten* (short coats). The concept of linked lateral stripes was introduced in the mid-Heian period.

129 ■ Tree Peony in Arabesque

The tree peony, the image the Chinese loved most, was embraced with equal affection by the Heian courtiers. Graceful *karakusa*, such as this one, often served as background designs for the equally graceful *kana* calligraphy, a highly regarded art form in itself.

130

130 ■ Japanese Tree Peony

Paintings of Chinese subjects executed in a Chinese style were called *kara-e;* Japanese subjects executed in a Japanese style were called *yamato-e.* Between these groups, there was a middle category—to which this design belongs— that contained elements of both, with a Chinese subject and a Japanese style. Taken from *emaki-mono,* this narrative painting emphasized thoughts and places dear to the hearts of the Japanese people, who viewed the scrolls in the company of good friends.

131

131 ■ Buddhist Flowers

Originally an image used only in Buddhist painting, the hibiscus was adopted into Heian culture early in the period and is shown here as a very modern, secular-looking design. As the Heian period matured, Buddhism became increasingly important; near the end of the period, a general sense of pessimism over the court's failure to control politics led to an even more fervent devotion to Buddhist tenets.

132 ■ Hibiscus
This highly stylized and unusual interpretation of *bussōge* (imaginary Buddhist
flowers that resemble hibiscus) was
designed to decorate *The Lotus Sutra* of
Heike *(Heike Nōgyō),* which was begun in
1164. The original design was painted in
gold on an indigo background.

133 ■ Scattered Pine Needles
The late Heian period is notorious for the
courtiers' obsession with their artistic
sensibilities. Such romanticism is apparent even in this seemingly simple pattern
of pine twigs, where the artist labored
long and hard to perfect the placement of
the motifs.

134

135

134 ■ Cranes Holding Pines
An auspicious pattern originally drawn in
gold and silver on lacquer with the *maki-e*
technique, this design focuses on the
much-loved images of the crane and the
pine. An enduring combination, cranes
and pines are still used today in celebra-
tions and weddings.

135 ■ Water Birds
Like example 20, this is an *ashide* (hidden
writing) pattern composed of birds, plants,
and moving streams. The composition
was made by a rubbing technique known
as *rōsen*, which created an illusion of light
and shade between the pattern and the
background, adding depth to the design.

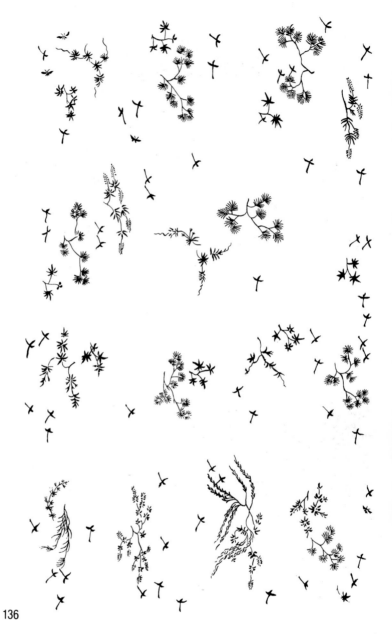

136

136 ■ Water Plants and Birds

This delicate design of birds and water plants first appeared in *The Anthology of the 36 Poets* as a *tsugi-shikishi*. *Tsugi-shikishi* is a kind of collage in which *ryōshi* (decorated papers) are torn or cut and then placed together in a composition. A popular technique during the Heian period, *tsugi-shikishi* heightened the opulence of the already elaborate poetry papers.

138

137 ■ Scattered Leaves

Komon (miniature patterns) were an inexpensive way to decorate textiles in the Heian period. This clean, simple composition of floating leaves works perfectly as a *komon* and was a popular design used in the decoration of clothing for the common people.

138 ■ Deer

Preserved today in the imperial repository at Shōsōin in Nara, this bilateral design of deer was made by a dyeing technique known as *kyōkechi* sometime between 710 and 785. A classic in both image and technique, this design is a dazzling example of the treasures of Shōsōin.

139

139 ■ Insects and Watermelons
In this lyrical design evoking dreams of
hot, steamy summer days, the watermelon chilling in a nearby stream is a
promise of a cooling repast. The artist has
humorously included insects in the
design, because they, too, are anticipating
the sweetness of the ripe watermelon.

140 ■ Maples
Used as a stencil design to decorate the
simple garments of commoners and
workers, this miniature pattern also
existed in much more elaborate court
versions. Some designs belonged exclusively to the aristocracy, but this maple
motif was widely used by all classes.

141

141 ■ Branded Horses

The brand was a slightly unconventional printing technique used during the Heian period. To create this pastoral design of grazing horses, the image was first carved on metal, then burned, and finally stamped ("branded") on paper.

142 ■ Snow Rings

At the close of the Heian period when the court began to lose power, the aristocracy became possessive of their patterns, preventing their use among other classes. The expense of the stencil cutting in this intricate design was enough to keep the pattern safe for the aristocrats.

143

144

143 ■ Diamonds

Considered in Heian times to be a high-toned design in excellent taste, this clever diamond-on-diamond pattern was first used to decorate the clothing and personal implements of the court nobility. Today, it can be seen in Shinto shrines as patterning on religious and sacred implements.

144 ■ Flowing Clouds

This early depiction of swirling clouds was probably brought to the Nara court from China. The flowing cloud pattern, which continued to gain popularity into the Heian period, was often used to decorate the back sides of hand mirrors.

145 ■ Flowing Water and Landscape
The bird's-eye perspective and strong diagonals used for this design were techniques borrowed from China's Northern Sung dynasty (960–1126). A wood engraving, the design is printed on *gubiki-shi,* a high-quality, handmade paper, and painted with crushed mother-of-pearl.

146 ■ Flowering *Karakusa*
As Japanese artists gained skill and confidence, they began to replace Chinese themes (like this arabesque) with their own cultural images. Literary themes were popular, as were referents to the four seasons and any display of *mono-no-aware* (sensitivity to the beauties of nature).

Descriptions of Color Plates

1 ■ Heian Court Scene
This fan-shaped picture narrative from a Heian handscroll aptly illustrates the variety of techniques used in these opulent works. The background is decorated with *karakami* and *maki-e*, and the figures are a combination of woodblock, *sumi*, and fine-line drawings in gold and silver.

2 ■ Scattered Trees and Birds
Clearly an early Heian work owing much of its style to the T'ang School, this carefully organized design has a vibrancy that makes it more than a carbon copy of Chinese art. Despite the rigid bilateralism, the freely drawn birds and easy scatterings of fruit and flowers give the design a character unusual for the time.

3 ■ Butterflies and Flowers
The delicately painted work of hibiscus and butterflies has a completely different character from the usual *karakusa* and roundel layout. The images here are drawn from top to bottom and arranged from left to right. The nobility probably admired both the intricacy of the refined pattern and the vibrancy of the complementary colors.

4 ■ Exotic Fruit in Arabesque
An exotic pattern depicting fruits from faraway lands, this design is an early version of the *karakusa* that originated in Persia and moved to Japan via the silk trail. The design can be found in nearly the same form today as a popular pattern used for *furoshiki* (cloth wrapper); it is also part of the costume used in the ritual lion dance known as *shishi-mai*.

5 ■ *Tsugi-shikishi*
A fragment from *The Anthology of the 36 Poets* shows the use of the popular Heian technique known as *tsugi-shikishi*, in which *ryōshi* (Japanese decorated papers) have been torn and collaged together to form a new design. The act of selecting and positioning the papers was considered an art in itself.

6 ■ *Seigaiha Tsugi-shikishi*
This beautiful collage shows three famous patterns, each created by a different technique. On the left is the most famous pattern, *seigaiha* (waves from the blue ocean). Within this design is the much-loved hemp leaf pattern, made by drawing the shape on gold paper and cutting it to fit within the arc of the *seigaiha*.

7 ■ Watermelon *Tsugi-shikishi*
This elaborate paper and gold leaf construction probably introduced the watermelon to the Nara court. Like *karakami* (Chinese decorated papers), the watermelon was an exotic import from China. Eventually, both the melon and the papers became domestic products.

8 ■ Tortoise Shell *Hanabashi*
The Heike *Lotus Sutra* was commissioned by Taira Kiyomori, the Heike military leader. The beautiful work was a conspicuous show of piety and expense, initiated to counter the popular attitude that the warrior class was both uncouth and uncultured. This elegant design at least speaks for the sophistication of the artisans and the wealth of Kiyomori and his warriors.

9 ■ *Zōgan* with Flowers
This refined design is taken from the back of a *biwa* (Japanese lute). The technique used is *zōgan*, a kind of marquetry in which the pattern is carved into a metal plate and inlaid with gold, silver, and wood.

10 ■ Heike Geometric
A total of 33 scrolls made up the Heike *Lotus Sutra*, which provided the finest examples of craftsmanship of the late Heian period, as this design attests. Part of *The Lotus Sutra* teaches that women who live by its tenets will be reborn on a

lotus within the blissful Amida Paradise.

11 ■ Scrolling Lotus
Strikingly contemporary, this design has clean lines and vibrant colors that set it apart from other Heian designs. The blue, green, and red lacquer are painted on a gold *maki-e* background; the pattern probably decorated a wedding chest.

12 ■ *Shishi* (Lion) and *Bussōge* (Imaginary Flowers)
The image of the lion was a tremendous favorite among the Heian courtiers. In this design, borrowed from China, the realistically drawn lion roars amid the classic *bussōge* (imaginary flowers that resemble hibiscus).

13 ■ Fish
Considering the intensity of the Heian period and its people, this nearly modern, cartoonlike design is a delightful surprise. The bird's-eye view of whimsical whales festooned in primary colors seems more Disney than Heian.

14 ■ Marquetry Roundels
The roundel in this design is the result of two processes: *zōgan* (silver, gold, and wood inlay on carved metal) for the pattern and *raden* (lacquer and mother-of-pearl inlay) for the delicate secondary motif.

15 ■ *Raden Bussōge*
Another opulent example of *raden*, the back of a nobleman's mirror has been intricately fitted with minute bits of mother-of-pearl and lacquerwork. An expensive and highly technical process, *raden* was used by the courtiers to decorate personal vanities, such as mirrors, and the back of the *biwa* (Japanese lute).

16 ■ Heian Court Pleasures
This wood engraving of Heian nobility engaged in the pursuit of refined pleasures nicely illustrates the way patterns were mixed together for proper court dress. For most occasions, under-robes—which could number up to 20—were arranged in a variegated rainbow of solid colored silks. The patterned outer-robes were blockprinted, woven, or embroidered.

■ GLOSSARY

Anthology of the 36 Poets A collection of poetry by 36 poets that was created to honor the Emperor Toba in 1112. Called *Sanjū Rokunin-Shū*, its 39 volumes were transcribed by 20 master calligraphers on decorated papers (*ryōshi*). This work of art stayed in the imperial family until the sixteenth century, when it was given to the Nishi Honganji Temple.

Ashide Also known as "hidden writing." A stylistic device characteristic of Heian art, particularly *yamato-e* works, in which *kana* script was ingeniously worked into the composition as an ornamental element. Used in painting, lacquerware, and decorated papers. The *kana* characters were often a kind of puzzle usually presented as *waka* (a short poem) relating to the artwork.

Asuka period Japanese historical era (552–710) tremendously influenced by the *Wei* and *Ch'i* cultures from China. Buddhism was introduced to Japan in 530; Prince Shotuku (592–622) established laws that followed Buddhist thought and principles. The Hōryūji Temple in Nara was constructed in the Asuka period.

Bussōge (Sometimes called *hossōge*.) An imaginary flower, resembling a hibiscus bloom, that was closely associated with Chinese Buddhism. Although the literal translation is "flowers of precious appearance," *bussōge* was sometimes called the T'ang motif because T'ang dynasty paintings of holy events often show these fantastic blossoms falling from heaven. The *bussōge* design came to Japan in the Nara period—along with Chinese imported papers (*karakami*)—where it was widely used as both a religious and a secular image.

Courtiers The aristocratic class of Heian-kyō, who resided exclusively within the walls of the capital city. This group of several hundred nobles, palace ladies, and members of the imperial family—usually connected to the throne by birth or marriage—constituted a highly refined, leisured, and literary elite. Aristocratic business for the courtiers consisted of an appreciation of proper protocol and etiquette and a mastery of poetry writing, calligraphy, and music. Elegance and sensitivity were much more important than military and political skills, which were generally considered to be necessary but uncouth talents. At its best, this obsession with aesthetic refinement (*miyobi*) resulted in a fusion of life and art and stimulated an outpouring of artistic treasures that made the Heian period the golden age of Japan.

Edo period Long, stable, and peaceful Japanese historical era (1603–1868). In 1590, military ruler Tokugawa Ieyasu centered his *bakafu* (tent headquarters) in the remote provincial center of Edo (present-day Tokyo). Eventually, the economic and cultural center of the country shifted from Kyoto/Osaka to the Tokyo plain. The Edo period, which was free of influence from abroad because all foreigners were banned, was noted for its openness and creativity in society and the arts. Popular literature and art flourished at this time.

Emaki-mono Literally, picture scrolls. Handscrolls that combined the finest artistic achievements of the Heian period, including *ryōshi* (decorated papers), painting, *kana* calligraphy, and poetry. *Yamato-e* (Japanese painting) flourished during the Heian period, largely because of the popularity of *emaki-mono*. A favorite social activity among the courtiers was the leisurely perusal of a new handscroll—a few inches at a time—with a few close friends. The making of *emaki-mono* was a joint effort that combined the color-placement and composition skills of the painting masters (*eshi*)—who were often members of the aristocracy—and the finishing work of the court artisans. The most famous example of *emaki-mono* is the tenth-century novel *The Tale of Genji*, which still exists in fragments.

Fujiwara era of the Heian period See "Heian period."

Fuki-nuki-yaki Literally, "blown-off-roof style," but popularly referred to as "bird's-eye perspective." Describes the Heian artistic device of removing ceilings from interior scenes so that the viewer seems to hover over the action. Typical of *onna-e* (domestic Heian painting), the *fuki-nuki-yaki* perspective was also used later in *onoko-e* (masculine paintings, usually with military and political themes).

Gagaku Elegant court music performed for its own sake or for the accompaniment of *bugaku* (court dances). Music was an important part of Heian life, and the courtiers were expected to be proficient on a variety of instruments, including the *biwa* and the *koto*.

Genji Tribal name of the Minamotos, a powerful military family that fought the Heike (Taira family) for control of the court in the late Heian period.

Gubiki-shi High-quality, handmade Japanese paper applied with crushed mother-of-pearl. These papers, usually used for *kana* calligraphy, are considered works of art in themselves.

Heian period Japanese historical era (794–1185) noted for its extraordinary concern for beauty, delicacy, and sensitivity in life and the arts. In 794, the imperial court moved from Nara to Heian-kyō (the capital of peace and tranquility), which was renamed Kyoto centuries later. Under the strong emperors Kammu and Saga during the early part of the Heian period (794–897), Japan maintained active relations with T'ang China. Then, as the powers of the emperors began to wane, one family of courtiers—the Fujiwaras—came to dominate affairs of state. After 894, communications with China were suspended, and the period from 897 to 1185 was called the late Heian, or Fujiwara, period. Japan then sought to develop its own artistic spirit. This shift of emphasis is clearly evident in the evolution of textile design and other arts.

Heike Tribal name for the Taira clan, a powerful military family led by Kiyomori.

The Heike took control of the imperial court in the later part of the Heian period. Ironically, the most important legacy of these military men was the exquisitely beautiful Heike *Lotus Sutra (Heike Nōgyō)*, commissioned by Kiyomori before the ultimate defeat of the Heike by their mortal enemies, the Genji (Minamotos).

Heike *Lotus Sutra* Thirty-three lavishly decorated scrolls of sutras dedicated to the principal deity of Itsukushima Shrine and commissioned by the Taira clan to counter the prevailing attitude that military tribes were uncouth, uncultured, and lacking in piety. In 1164, each member of the clan undertook the preparation of a scroll and engaged the finest talents in Heian-kyō in an effort to outdo one another. In creating *The Lotus Sutra*, which is generally held to be the finest example of the period's artwork, the Heike had beaten the aristocracy at their own culture game.

Inkin Literally, stamped gold. A process in which gold leaf is directly applied or stamped onto the cloth.

Kamakura period Japanese historical era (1185–1338) noted for its militaristic character. The artistically brilliant Heian period ended in 1185, when, after years of conflict, the Minamoto family defeated the rival Taira family, and military families began their rise to power. Although the imperial court remained in Kyoto, its influence was lessened, and Kamakura in eastern Japan was chosen as the seat of the shogunate. In the arts, the intricate and delicate Heian patterns gave way to the more practical camouflage patterns used to cover armor.

Kammu Emperor of Japan from 781 to 806, who moved the capital of the country from Nara to Kyoto in 794.

Kana Japanese syllabic writing, often cited as the most important achievement of the highly cultured Heian period. The *kana* syllabary was invented by Kōbō Daishi and further developed by the women of the court in response to the inadequacies and taboos of *kanji*, the ideographs adopted from China. Written *kanji* was for the exclusive use of Heian males, who completely excluded the literary-minded females of the court from its teaching. Initially, the 48 *kana* characters were used to express the intimacies of domestic life within the court, appearing in diaries, *waka* poetry, and the full-blown tales of *monogatari*. *Kana* calligraphy, also known as grass script, became an art form in its own right and was regarded with the respect accorded to paintings, lacquerware, and handmade decorated papers. *Kana* was soon adopted by the men of the court.

Kanji The Chinese system of writing composed of ideographs in which each character represents a specific idea. First used in China in 14 B.C., the language was systematized by the time it reached Japan by way of Korea in the fifth century. Initially, *kanji* was taught only to male children, causing it to develop as a public language associated with political and military concerns. Today, *kanji* is one of the three written languages taught throughout Japan. To read a newspaper with complete comprehension, it is said, the reader must recognize and understand ten thousand *kanji* characters.

Kanzeha A swelling-wave pattern that appears in many Japanese designs.

Kara-e Literally, Chinese painting. Paintings in the Chinese style with Chinese themes (usually referring to the art of the T'ang dynasty). As opposed to *yamato-e* paintings, which contain distinctively Japanese style and subject matter.

Karakami Elegant decorated paper originally imported from China to Japan during the Heian period. Also known as Chinese paper, it was made by covering select *torinoko* paper with *gofun* (lime) and printing the design in mica. Highly prized in ancient Japanese society, *karakami* provided the inspiration for the development of Japan's own cultural traditions.

Karakusa Literally, scrolling vine. A sequential pattern that is systematically organized so it can be endlessly expanded. An arabesque motif particularly characteristic of Heian patterns, *karakusa* can be traced from Persia to India, China, Korea, and finally Japan.

Kara-nishiki Silk brocade woven in China and imported into Japan during the Nara and early Heian periods. See example 51.

Komon Literally, miniature patterns. The patterns can be quite large, for some reason, and still be called *komon*. Widely appreciated during the Heian period, *komon* reached the zenith of popularity in the Edo period, when master stencil cutters designed blades that enabled the artists to expand their repertory of designs.

Kyōkechi Resist dyeing done with woodblocks or boards.

Maki-e Literally, sprinkled picture. A late-Heian technique for decorating lacquerware in which gold and silver particles were sprinkled onto moist lacquer to achieve the design. Each lacquer layer—often 40 or more—was then sanded to even the surface and bring out the luster.

Minamoto See "Genji."

Monogatari Tales or literature.

Nara period Japanese historical era (710–794) in which Japan was united for the first time. The period was named after the city of Nara, which is considered the ancient-ancient capital of Japan (Kyoto is the ancient capital). During this period, the Japanese were deeply influenced socially and artistically by Buddhism and T'ang dynasty China.

Obi A sash or cummerbund worn with kimono. There are as many kind of *obi* as there are fabrics, colors, and designs. The correct *obi* choice depends on the kimono, the season, the occasion, and the wearer's marital status. Often hand-woven, the *obi* itself is a work of art.

Raden Lacquer and mother-of-pearl inlay. Often used to decorate lacquerware.

Rōsen A printing technique used to transfer designs and patterns onto handmade papers that were then used for *waka* poetry.

Ryōshi Japanese decorated papers.

Shikishi Handmade, almost-square sheets of painted or printed paper that were used as a ground for calligraphy and poetry.

Shintoism Literally, "the way of the gods." The native religion of Japan, based on the virtues of simplicity, purity, and cleanliness. In contrast to Buddhism, which entered Japanese culture in the Nara period, Shintoism is an optimistic, positive religion that teaches a reverence for nature. Followers of Shintoism believe that God inhabits all living things in the form of *kami* (spirits), who are worshipped in and out of Shinto shrines. The later spread of Confuciansim and Buddhism lessened the influence of Shintoism, but the religion is still important in Japanese life; a large part of what we admire as "typically Japanese" is based in Shintoism.

Shōsōin The imperial repository in Nara that houses ten thousand objects and personal effects from the Nara period.

Sumi-e Black-and-white ink painting.

Sung dynasty, Northern Chinese historical era (960–1126), which paralleled Japan's Heian period. More introspective than the extroverted T'ang dynasty that was the inspiration for most of Heian culture, the Sung dynasty is best known for its monochromatic ink landscapes. Still, many artistic devices that were important characteristics of Heian art—subdued color tones, bird's-eye perspective, stress upon the diagonal plane—can be traced back to the Sung aesthetic.

Sutra A Buddhist prayer, either written or chanted.

Taira See "Heike."

Tale of Genji (Genji Monogatari) A romance of classical Japanese court life written in the Heian period by Lady Murasaki Shikibu. Considered the first novel ever written, the 54 chapters were originally contained within 20 separate scrolls with hundreds of illustrations and thousands of sheets of calligraphy. Only surviving now in fragments, *Genji* has been an inspiration as a work of art in all respects through the centuries.

T'ang dynasty Chinese historical era (618–906) known for its artistic creativity and cultural achievements. This was the golden age of Chinese poetry and the time of China's greatest influence on Korea and Japan.

Tsugi-shikishi A Heian technique in which decorated papers are torn and collaged together to form a new design.

Waka Japanese poetry, each poem consisting of 31 syllables, written in *kana* script. *Waka* and *emaki-mono* were among the most important cultural achievements of the Heian period. The clandestine passing of *waka* poems was the preferred means of communication between the courtiers, who disliked direct communication. The making of this poetry was also an important social activity with the courtiers, who displayed their syllabic skills with the same intensity and enthusiasm that we might play tennis. The Heian aristocrat was far more likely to be judged by his poetic abilities than by his military talents.

Yamato-e Paintings of Japanese subjects in a distinctively Japanese style. As opposed to the T'ang style that was predominant in the Nara period and early Heian period, *yamato-e* was a domestic art that dealt primarily with poetic subject matter—such as seasonal changes, the romance of court life, and the beauty of a flowing stream, a soaring bird, or other subject matter that we now regard as "typically Japanese."

Yūsoku Intricate, exotic court patterns that were specifically designed for use on ceremonial garments worn at the Heian court. These designs were the exclusive property of the Heian aristocracy; commoners were not permitted to wear them.

Zōgan The art of inlay. A kind of marquetry in which the pattern is carved onto a plate and inlaid with gold, silver, and wood. In the Fujiwara era, it was applied not only to wood and metal, but also to silk cloth. The gold leaf was cut out in a fine design and applied to the textile with lacquer. *Zōgan* is similar to the damascene process used by metalworkers today.

BIBLIOGRAPHY

Baker, Joan Stanley. *Japanese Art*. London: Thames and Hudson, Ltd., 1984.

Collcutt, Martin, Marius Jansen, and Isao Kamakura. *Cultural Atlas of Japan*. New York: Facts on File, Inc., 1988.

Hempel, Rose. *The Golden Age of Japan*. New York: Rizzoli, 1983.

Minnish, Helen Benton. *Japanese Costume*. Rutland, Vt., and Tokyo: Charles E. Tuttle Co., 1963.

Murase, Miyeko. *Tales of Japan*. New York and Oxford: Oxford University Press, 1986.

Puette, William J. *Guide to "The Tale of Genji."* Rutland, Vt., and Tokyo: Charles E. Tuttle Co., 1983.

Seattle Art Museum. *A Thousand Cranes*. San Francisco: Chronicle Books, 1987.

Shikibu, Murasaki. *The Tale of Genji*. Translated by Edward G. Seidensticker. New York: Alfred A. Knopf, 1976.

Yoshikawa, Eiji. *The Heike Story*. Translated by Fuki Wooyenaka Uramatsu. Rutland, Vt., and Tokyo: Charles E. Tuttle Co., 1956.